ESSE

Help Your 7-
Read Better

Parents' essentials – friendly books for busy parents
to help their children fulfil their potential.

For full details please send for a free copy of the latest catalogue.
See back cover for address.

Help Your 7–11 Year Old Read Better

Ken Adams

PARENTS' ESSENTIALS

Published in 2001 by
How To Books Ltd, 3 Newtec Place,
Magdalen Road, Oxford OX4 1RE, United Kingdom
Tel: (01865) 793806   Fax: (01865) 248780
email: info@howtobooks.co.uk
www.howtobooks.co.uk

British Library Cataloguing in Publication Data.
A catalogue record for this book is available from
the British Library.

Cover design by Shireen Nathoo Design
Produced for How To Books by Deer Park Productions
Typeset by PDQ Typesetting, Newcastle-under-Lyme, Staffordshire
Printed and bound in Great Britain by The Baskerville Press Ltd.

NOTE: The material contained in this book is set out in good faith
for general guidance and no liability can be accepted for loss or
expense incurred as a result of relying in particular circumstances
on statements made in the book. Laws and regulations are complex
and liable to change, and readers should check the current position
with the relevant authorities before making personal arrangements.

ESSENTIALS *is an imprint of*
How To Books

Contents

Preface

From being able to read simple stories to reading and understanding more complex stories is a big jump for the seven to eleven-year-old age group. The secret of success is basically to read, read and read even more. However, there are many ways of stimulating interest and of improving reading skills. Building such skills systematically through a progressive, step-wise reading scheme is one way. This builds confidence and promotes an interest in reading if the stories are both imaginative and, especially for young readers, well illustrated. There is a progressive line drawn from large-type, brightly-coloured picture books to adventure stories with few pictures but good story content for this age group.

In addition, comprehensive exercises, word and sentence-building, and puzzles and games, both stimulate and help the reading process. There is much to learn, but with good organisation and emphasis on the enjoyment of reading, progress at this primary age can be considerable. The purpose of this book is to show you how to build on early reading activities and produce a competent and knowledgeable reader.

Ken Adams

1 Methods for Improving Reading

By the age of seven, most children are reading well enough to enjoy stories for themselves. For most, though, these are very simple stories. The level of understanding needed is not very great, and one purpose of reading activities over the next few years is to raise the level of awareness of word and sentence meanings. This can best be done in context, but learning principles can be employed to build on what a child already knows, through supplementary activities.

It is important to establish first the level of word recognition and understanding that a learner has reached before trying to progress any further. This can be achieved by various means – through reading tests, hearing a child read, simple comprehension tests and even word puzzles and games. Once a clear idea of the learner's attainment has been gained, the building process can begin.

STEP-WISE LEARNING

The central idea of sequenced or step-wise learning is that, once a child's attainment is established, they can progress in ability by small, graded steps. Any attempt to build by taking short cuts, or jumping up several steps at a time, from simple things to the more complex, often results in failure and discouragement. Therefore, it is very important that reading activities are graded in some way, so that a child is successful and is kept motivated. This is especially important for slow learners.

Fast learners may be able to progress through a confused scenario, when a mixture of simple and difficult reading work is presented. Average and slow learners, however, need careful staging of activities to progress at a maximum rate. Even fast learners benefit from careful ordering of activities, although to produce a programme of step-wise learning in reading is notoriously difficult because of the complex nature of reading, and of reading texts in particular. Reading does not just involve recognition of words, it also includes understanding word meanings, sentence meanings, the events in a story or a passage of writing, and, at a higher level, inferences.

FROM THE CONCRETE TO THE ABSTRACT

Increasingly, as a reader moves on from picture books to reading novels, or factual writing, they will be faced with the transition from thinking in terms of concrete words and ideas, to attempting to understand so-called abstract words and thoughts. Whereas, for example, a six-year-old reads about real-life objects and actions, the well-read older child or adult will be thinking in terms of emotions and even higher ideas. This is the gap that needs to be bridged.

In addition, motivation to read must be kept strong. There is little point in applying rigorous 'turned off' reading and writing. Effective progress can be achieved at the beginning by mixing simple picture stories with slightly more difficult reading pieces, simple comprehension with puzzles and word searches, and word building exercises with spelling and grammar. It is very important at all levels of understanding to stress word meanings, so simple sentence building will help to explain word meanings by looking at their context. For example, 'The king *reigns* over the country'.

2 Finding a Basic Level to Build On

This chapter and others will include reading tests (recognition of words), graded passages for reading, and graded comprehension exercises to help you assess your child's level of reading attainment and then build on it. If your child's knowledge of phonics is poor, it is essential that you concentrate for a period on improving this area of reading.

READING TESTS

These are essentially tests of word recognition. They do not give any idea of knowledge of word meanings or of the level of ability to understand sentence meaning or the events in a story.

The following words are only a guide to a reading level. They are not standardised tests, but move from words with a simple phonic structure to words with a considerably more complex structure.

Phonics

cat	dog	man
tap	hat	bag
pen	pin	bus
sun	lip	mug
jam	fat	rat
kid	lid	net

vet	win	box
yet	zip	queen
blot	brick	spoon
clip	crab	
drop	egg	
frog	grip	
flag	pram	
glad	step	
plug	skip	
scan	trip	
spot	sock	
slip	shop	
swim	that	
tree	moon	
chip	feet	
foot	king	
dust	rush	

end   kill

door   queen

Up to this point the words you are asking your child to read have a phonic basis, although words like 'door' do not. If a reader experiences great difficulty in this section, then phonics will have to be re-learnt (see *Help Your Child Read Well, 5–7 Years*, in this series).

Word building on phonics, and other simple words

Extended phonic words include 'sitting' or 'tennis', both using 'short' vowels.

Some simple words, used much by children in stories, have 'long' vowels or other sounds for vowels, including 'ball', 'old', 'was'. Combinations of vowels cause difficulty, too – 'sea', 'out'.

Get your child to try the following words. They may seem simple to you, but some early readers have difficulty with them:

ball	small	gold
spring	wash	her
she	they	what
sky	game	out
about	you	your
read	cart	pull

clean	jar	morning
play	white	away
every	boat	nice
bread	school	have
pay	hole	said
paper	were	count
mouth	nose	mother
father	winter	summer
sister	table	dinner
water	letter	show
first	chair	fairy
pretty	grass	each
only	talk	horse
cold	after	mouse
year	more	lady

Being able to read the above words would suggest that a child has a basic ability in reading of about seven years of age.

Further words usually read by fairly good readers of seven or eight years

swing	stick	brave
spoon	street	paint
grandad	myself	children
another	teacher	window
bedroom	garden	farmer
church	burn	night
firework	stairs	outside
talking	asking	reading
football	party	dance
stories	today	tomorrow
anything	nothing	behind
sound	learn	number
uncle	aunt	blue
orange	one	two
eight	Wednesday	Saturday
July	August	February
rainbow	money	needle

proud	pear	prince
princess	field	monkey
chicken	understand	yellow
someone	candle	lamb
dirty	Christmas	young
quickly	writing	afraid
yesterday	afternoon	birthday
sugar	friend	hundred
wolf	half	knife
railway	building	question
answer	history	

This is not a complete list because very good readers have a much wider bank of words in their memory that they will recognise. However, these three lists give a good guide.

For example, a child of seven or eight years who reads these words easily can happily be taken at speed through the exercises and reading matter in this book. A reader who stumbles frequently needs a patient hand in further reading work.

More difficult words for your child to read

property	always	altogether
kitchen	mountain	kangaroo

castle	newspaper	midnight
adventure	holiday	cabbage
beautiful	dangerous	monster
forgotten	potatoes	tomatoes
beginning	remember	entertain
arithmetic	biology	passenger
information	disappear	wonderful
telephone	electric	imagination
gentleman	accident	invitation
examination	pavement	population
department	umbrella	hospital
century	lightning	million
elephant	geography	conductor
determination	introduction	

This chapter represents a beginning – finding out what words a child can read.

Further chapters need to establish knowledge of word meanings, sentence meanings and the understanding of a range of written passages. Such work can also help to improve the reading of a learner.

3 Reading Stories

By the time children are seven or eight there is a very wide diversity in ability to read. You, as a parent or teacher, will need to know if your child can just marginally be called a reader, or is very competent indeed at reading. For example, John at seven years had been reading well for many years and was only one year off taking and passing a GCSE exam. Richard, on the other hand, at the same age, could just recognise a few words and had a vague idea of a story line from accompanying pictures. To help you have a clear idea of your child's reading ability several reading passages are included below with questions you can ask about the story line.

LEVEL 1 – KEN GETS WET

Today is a hot day. Ken, the dog, runs down to the river. He sees a fish in the water. The fish is very fast. It swims away, and Ken falls in the river with a big splash! Ken is happy. He can swim, and the water is warm.

Questions to ask

1 Where does Ken go?
2 What does Ken see?
3 Why does Ken fall in the water?
4 Is he sad at the end?

Get your child to read the above to you and answer your questions. At this age, they should be very confident with this level of reading.

LEVEL 2 – THE BEAR AT THE BOTTOM OF THE GARDEN

One day, Mary went to her Grandma's house. At the end of the garden she found a tree with a small house in it. She knocked on the door and a small Bear opened it.

'Hello,' said the Bear, 'I am Wally Wimbush. I am famous.'

'I've never heard of you,' said Mary.

The Bear waved Mary into the house.

'Lots of people have heard of me,' he said. 'Do you want tea? I have lots of tea for all the people who come to visit.'

He sat down, put his feet on the table, and picked up the tea-pot with his toes. Then he poured the tea into a cup.

'It's not very nice, you know,' said Mary, 'putting your feet on the table.'

'Stufflepots!' said Wally, 'It is very, very polite to put your feet on the table.'

Questions to ask

1 What did Mary find at her Grandma's?
2 Who was famous?
3 What was there lots of?
4 What is *not* polite?

LEVEL 3 – SAMANTHA SAVED THE WORLD TODAY

Samantha saved the World today,
While she was going out to play.
Down by the village cricket ground
She found a Giant stamping round.
On seeing her, he gave a roar

And moved to crush her to the floor.
Samantha did not seem to care,
Just fixed the Giant with a stare.
And in a second, in a wink,
The Monster Man began to shrink,
Until, when smaller than the hay,
The tiny Giant ran away.

Questions to ask

1 What did Samantha save as she was playing?
2 What did Samantha find at the village cricket ground?
3 What did Samantha do to save herself? (A little word here.)
4 What happened to Samantha's enemy at the end?

LEVEL 4 – PETER AND THE POLTI

It seemed just like any other morning when Peter came down
to eat his breakfast. Mum was in the kitchen busy burning the
toast. Peter's big sister, Lisa, was rushing around screaming,
'Where are my clean socks?'

The dog was in his usual place, hiding under the table
with his paws stuck in his ears, and Grandma was sitting in the
only comfy armchair, busily knitting a Gorilla-sized jumper for
baby Cousin Netta in Australia.

Peter sat quietly down at the breakfast table, and tried to
ignore all the madness going on around him; but it was no
use. 'Get out of my way!' shrieked his sister, pushing him aside
to grab the last piece of burnt toast. Suddenly, Peter felt
depressed. Today was turning out to be even worse than usual.

Perhaps he was going to starve to death as well as having to
go to school.

Then, the miracle happened. The tomato sauce bottle on
the table in front of him began to move. Slowly, it rose into
the air, unscrewed its own top, and moved until it was directly
above the horrible Lisa. Then, it turned itself upside down and
shook the red, gooey mess all over Lisa's silky, blonde hair.
'A r r r h!', she gasped as the ooze slipped down her face and
on to her clean, white blouse.

Peter watched open-mouthed, as the tomato sauce bottle
screwed its own top back on, and put itself right way up on
the table again.

'Now,' said Peter to himself, 'perhaps today will be a good
day after all.'

Questions to ask

1   What was happening in the kitchen?
2   Why was the dog hiding under the table?
3   What was wrong with the jumper Grandma was knitting?
4   What happened that was very unusual?
5   Find a word that means that Peter was feeling fed up.
7   How did Peter *feel* at the end of the story?

The above reading pieces, plus the short comprehension
questions, give an idea of the level at which a child is working
and thinking. If he or she can easily both read the passages
and answer the questions, then the level of understanding is
good. To build on such attainment will not be too difficult,
and motivation will be high.

A reader who stumbles, and shows lack of comprehension from the very beginning needs much understanding and help from an adult.

4 Building on What is Already Known

To improve reading over this age group requires attention to several aspects.

WORDS

A child needs to recognise words in text, but must also be aware of the meanings of those words in their contexts. For example, they may need to recognise the word, 'together', but also how this works in the text – what is 'together' in the story?

SENTENCES

A child may be able to *read* all the words in a sentence but the meaning of the sentence can be totally lost on them. This may partly be because individual word meanings are only dimly understood, but also because the overall sentence meaning is lost. A sentence like, 'She quickly ran through the contents of the wardrobe' to a small child can mean actually running through the wardrobe, rather than the true meaning.

The meaning of a paragraph or passage can also be lost on a young reader. Sometimes passages need to be read over several times.

This, and the following sections of this chapter, will extend the knowledge of word structure and meaning, of sentence construction and meaning, and of the understanding of whole passages.

WORDS AND THEIR MEANINGS

Meanings of words can be learnt partly through reading text, but also very effectively by simple exercises in opposites, analogies, words in the right place (in a sentence), and in other word exercises.

Level 1

At this basic level, simple words only are used.

Opposites

What is the opposite of:

day_____   bad_____

up_____   thin_____

cold_____   shut_____

new_____

Choose from:

down   fat   good

hot   open   old

night

Sounds

What makes these sounds:

bow-wow_____   moo_____

tick-tock_____   quack_____

me-ow_____

Choose from:

cat	dog	duck
cow	clock	

Words out of place

Underline the word which is the odd one out.

1 dog   cat   ship   cow   rabbit

2 man   boy   cup   girl   mum

3 spoon   cup   foot   mug   plane

4 nose   eye   hair   car   foot

What is wrong?

1 I am a dog. I live in the sea.

2 I am a fish. I eat chips for dinner.

3 I am a duck. I live on the Moon.

Words with similar meanings

Choose from these words the words which are nearly the same:

start   hole   look

quick   fall   little

drop_____ begin_____ gap_____

see_____ fast_____ small_____

Level 2

Opposites

Choose from:

soft   many   light   high

empty   white   buy   dirty

dry   friend   small   bottom

dark_____ black_____ full_____

few_____ low_____ clean_____

wet_____ sell_____ hard_____

enemy_____ big_____ top_____

Sounds

Choose from:

hoot   slam   bang   drip

the_____ of a door

the_____ of a gun

the_____ of a horn

the_____ of a tap

Jobs

Choose from:

clown   doctor   policeman   teacher

I help children in a school. I am a_____

I make people laugh. I am a_____

I work in a hospital. I am a_____

I help the traffic along. I am a_____

Words similar in meaning
Choose from:

shining   circular   constable

difficult   emperor   halt

policeman_____   bright_____

round_____   hard_____

king_____   stop_____

Levels 3 and 4

Opposites
Choose from:

alive   answer   arrive   asleep

beautiful   expensive   live   multiply

entrance   first   quiet   poor

short   there   front   friend

fast   wrong   young

awake_____   ugly_____

die_____   enemy_____

question_____   depart_____

dead_____   divide_____

exit_____   cheap_____

last_____   slow_____

back_____   old_____

right_____   here_____

tall_____   rich_____

noisy_____

Sounds
Choose from:

chains   whip   water

bell   steam   feet

corks   telephone

_____ bubbles _____ chimes

_____ patter   _____ pop

_____ rings   _____ clank

_____ cracks   _____ hisses

Jobs

What am I? Choose from:

pilot   postman   mechanic   chemist

optician   dentist   plumber   grocer

I give out medicines in a shop_____

I fly an aeroplane_____

I test eyesight_____

I look after people's teeth_____

I mend burst pipes_____

I mend cars_____

I sell food_____

I deliver letters_____

What is wrong?
1 The man was as tall as he was as a baby.
2 I had 10 sweets. I gave 3 away. I had 20 left.
3 'I am deaf and dumb,' said the boy.
4 'I have counted thirty four horses in this field,' said the blind man.
5 'I am going to the football match that took place last Saturday.'
6 The girl put salt on her ice-cream to make it sweeter.

The above exercises will help to reinforce a child's reading and understanding abilities, and can help their reading to progress.

5 Further Improvements in Reading

Comprehension exercises provide good reading practice, and also aim to improve understanding. This section has graded exercises for a child to work through.

RED RIDING HOOD

There was this wolf and a little girl. They lived in a wood. One day, Red's mum told her to go down to her Nan's house, so she went and the wolf followed her. He got there first, and pretended to be a grandma. Red didn't recognise her, because grandma looked a bit like a wolf anyway. Where the grandma went I don't know. She probably went down the bingo. Then the wolf tried to swallow Red, but his teeth were too big. Then someone came, probably a cop or something, and chopped off the wolf's head, and they all lived happily ever after. I think so anyway but it is all very boring.

(Samson Superslug)

1 Who is Red?
2 Where did this boy think grandma was?
3 Why could the wolf not swallow Red?
4 Who did the boy think came to chop off the wolf's head?
   (Choose from a dragon, a prince, a policeman, a teacher.)
5 What did the boy think of the story?

THE GHOST KILLER GANG

It began at school the very next day with Rebecca Fox. Rebecca was in our class, and she was weird, real weird. It wasn't that she looked particularly strange, in fact, she looked sweet. Like an Angel really. She had bubbles of curly blonde hair, big blue eyes and a tiny face like an elf. She was teacher's favourite, definitely.

But she was odd. She had a faraway look in her eyes as though she was in some other land. She never talked to anyone, except to answer a question.

'It's like she's hypnotised,' said Sue, 'standing on her own like that at break-time.'

'And has anyone seen her after school?' asked Sol.

'She goes home with her grandma,' I said. 'They live in that big house at the bottom of High Street, just her and her grandma.'

I knew that because I'd once had a paper round at that end of town, but I'd given it up. All those big, spooky houses put me off. They looked like great spiders in the early morning, ready to pounce. So I chickened out, and stayed in bed instead.

One day, in the classroom, our teacher, 'Beaky', told us to get on with writing a story, and we three each kept half an eye on Rebecca.

Suddenly, Sol leaned across and whispered: 'Look at Rebecca.'

I looked to my left, where she was busy writing her story. At first, I could see nothing strange about what she was doing; she seemed to be doing what she did best – being a good pupil.

Then, I realised that her writing hand was not moving, but resting on the table, absolutely still. At the same time her pen, half hidden by motionless, outstretched fingers, was writing away merrily on its own! I gasped, and looked across at Sue. Her eyes were also fixed intently on the dancing pen.

'Incredible!' whispered Sol to me.

1 How many friends are there watching Rebecca? Give the names of two of them.
2 What word describes Rebecca – ugly, fat, giant, sweet, ferocious?
3 Describe the house in which Rebecca lives.
4 Did Rebecca talk a lot?
5 What does Sue think is the matter with her?
6 What does the writer think the big houses look like in the early morning? Explain.
7 What was happening in the writing lesson that was very unusual indeed?
8 Try to give an explanation for the happenings in this story.

WHEN I WAS YOUR AGE
Sammy emptied his money-box on to the kitchen table.

'I've got two pounds left from my birthday money,' he said, 'and one pound of pocket money to come. I can buy something good with all that.'

'When I was your age,' said grandpa, 'I was so rich that for my mother's birthday I bought her a Rolls-Royce, one hundred beautiful dresses and a castle, with just half of one week's pocket money. That's how rich I was.'

'I don't think so,' said Sammy.

On Tuesday, Sammy wasn't feeling hungry at tea-time.

'I had three helpings of rice pudding for dinner today,' he said. 'I'm still full up.'

'When I was your age,' said Grandpa, 'I used to eat six bowls of porridge, twenty sausages, ten rashers of bacon with fifteen fried eggs, and eleven pieces of toast, and drink three jugs of milk, just for breakfast. That's how good I was at eating.'

'I don't think so,' said Sammy.

On Wednesday, Sammy played in the school football team. 'I scored the winning goal,' he told Grandpa. 'I got the Man of the Match award.'

'When I was your age,' said Grandpa, 'I was the only one in the school team. I played defence, attack and goalkeeper and I won all the matches twenty-five to nil. That's how good I was at football.'

'I don't think so,' said Sammy.

On Thursday, Grandpa collected Sammy from school.

'Oh, I am tired,' said Sammy. 'It's such a long walk home after a hard day's work.'

'When I was your age,' said Grandpa, 'I had to get up in the middle of the night, walk fifty miles to school, through crocodile-infested swamps and over the highest mountain in the country, carrying my school books and my little sister on my back, that's how good I was at walking.'

'I don't think so,' said Sammy.

1 Explain why Sammy keeps on saying, 'I don't think so'.
2 How do you know that Grandpa was supposed to be rich?
3 Why is it especially difficult to believe that Grandpa can eat

as much as he says?

4 What does the word 'exaggeration' mean? Explain how this fits with what Grandpa says.

5 Why is it very difficult for Grandpa to be the only one in the school team playing against a full team of eleven?

6 How long do you think it would take Grandpa to walk 50 miles to school and 50 miles back? Why does this make what Grandpa says impossible?

6 Sentences and More Difficult Reading Work

Word and sentence meanings are extended below for the learner who is, or becomes, competent from previous reading and exercises.

WORD BUILDING

Nouns, adjectives and verbs can be built from other words. This section helps with recognising words, not necessarily with understanding meanings.

Add these endings to the following words

-or	-ment	-ence	-ning
-ion	-hood	-ness	-ren
-liness	-ure	-y	-ity
-hood	-ship	-father	-ation
-ice	-ous	-al	-lion
-ance	-ster	-ness	-like

war_____ young_____ sick_____

attend_____ rebel_____ music_____

mountain_____ just_____ inform_____

grand_____ friend_____ false_____

equal_____   discover_____   depart_____

clean_____   child_____   bright_____

boy_____   collect_____   light_____

exist_____   act_____   advertise_____

Form compound words from the following

ache   ball   church   cup

fire   butter   gentle   lamp

life   school   thrift   strong

cloth   house

Fit with these words:

_____fly _____stand _____ guard

_____teacher_____board_____ yard

foot_____   heart_____   _____man

spend_____   head_____   _____maid

table_____   _____man

OPPOSITES

Finding opposites can be very effective in sorting out the meanings of words. The following opposites are more difficult than in previous work.

Find the opposites of these words:

absence_____	accept_____
difficult_____	backward_____
bright_____	coarse_____
educated_____	enemy_____
everywhere_____	famous_____
guilty_____	height_____
inferior_____	permanent_____
shallow_____	opaque_____
pleasant_____	private_____
retreat_____	south_____
straight_____	success_____
summer_____	vague_____
contract_____	maximum_____
morning_____	narrow_____

selfish_____   west_____

singular_____   victory_____

wax_____   wealth_____

Choose from:

minimum	broad	east	deep
refuse	presence	easy	unknown
friend	uneducated	nowhere	innocent
depth	temporary	advance	unpleasant
transparent	public	smooth	forward
dull	superior	bent	expand
north	failure	definite	plural
winter	afternoon	unselfish	poverty
wane	defeat		

MORE DIFFICULT WORDS WITH SIMILAR MEANINGS

Put the correct words together:

abode_____	leave_____
plentiful_____	accused_____
sharp_____	adhere_____
enemy_____	elude_____
calamity_____	deceive_____
bravery_____	sly_____
talk_____	comprehend_____
commence_____	conceal_____
circular_____	astonish_____
wonder_____	assemble_____
ancient_____	caution_____
broad_____	enormous_____
exterior_____	interior_____
heroic_____	imitate_____
margin_____	mariner_____
swamp_____	meagre_____

moisture_____   peculiar_____

odour_____   rowdy_____

agile_____   profit_____

prompt_____   guard_____

purchase_____   ramble_____

rank_____   regret_____

remedy_____   street_____

wander_____   stubborn_____

surrender_____   suspended_____

clear_____   tranquil_____

vacant_____   sufficient_____

wretched_____   annually_____

Choose from:

dampness	protect	buy
road	position	yield
yearly	obstinate	copy
outside	inside	gain

dwelling	abandon	round
surprise	gather	amazement
old	care	wide
gigantic	hide	begin
conversation	understand	cunning
courage	cheat	disaster
escape	foe	stick
acute	noisy	smell
marsh	sailor	brave
edge	scanty	nimble
strange	sorrow	roam
hung	peaceful	transparent
walk	empty	miserable
cure	quick	blamed
abundant	enough	

TURNING WORDS INTO SENTENCES

Choose from these words to go into the sentences below:

explained   shouted   pleaded

answered   bled   stopped

ended   closed   beautiful

frowned   whispered   mumbled

His watch_____at nine o'clock.

The story_____.

The door_____.

It was a_____garden.

He_____softly.

She_____indistinctly.

The headmaster_____angrily.

John_____why he was late.

He_____with joy.

The prisoner_____for mercy.

'That is right,' he_____.

The soldier_____profusely.

7 Fitting Words and Phrases into Sentences

The following chapters are from a book called *The Ghost Killer Gang*. Fitting words and phrases into the story is a good exercise for readers of this age. It encourages reading, and helps a learner to select the best words and phrases for a storyline.

In *The Ghost Killer Gang* story there are three main characters:

Soloman, Sue and a Kid named Blue, all aged about eleven. Roger is a dog belonging to Blue.

Exercise 1

It all happened one _____ morning.

Every day just before school I hop over the fence at the bottom of our garden and give our dog, Roger, a run in the fields. Usually, I just stand and watch him, running around like crazy, looking for rabbits. After about ten minutes, he comes back, looking for his breakfast and _____ button.

This day, though, Roger didn't come back. He just

_____.

The thing is, I can see for miles across those fields – there's not a bush in sight. Only an old ruin almost totally flattened, about a quarter of a mile away.

That morning, I stood and yelled myself hoarse for five minutes, then trotted across to the ruins. This was all I needed to happen on a school day!

Roger, who was well known for being the Artful Dodger and dodging off down rabbit holes, was putting me in deadly danger from Mrs Proops our Headmistress, who had a special face for latecomers, a face that could _____ a forest fire. Better to brave The Sahara Desert or The Amazon Jungle than face Mrs Proops when you were late!

I reached the stonework in the centre of the field, and called out again.

'Roger! You Dodger! Come here! You're going to get me hung, drawn and chopped into little pieces!'

Then I stood and listened. There was nothing. Only the wind blowing dust across the ruins. No space or hole for even Roger to _____ down.

I called again. And again. Still no Roger.

Then I gave it up and went home.

'He'll be back,' said Mum, 'Roger's a Dodger, but he's no wanderer.'

That was true. Roger liked home comforts. If he was a human being, he'd wear slippers and have cups of hot chocolate before going off to bed. He was _____ , but also a soppy, sloppy dog. Roger was no _____. He would never, ever, be the first dog up Mount Everest.

I went to school, and the first person I bumped into was Solomon, who was sitting in the corner of the playground reading some book almost as big as he was.

'The ruins,' he said, looking at me over the top of his specs. 'Now, that's interesting. Very interesting.'

'What's interesting?' I asked. There was only a field with a few stones, and a dog called Roger, hiding in a rabbit hole.

How was that interesting?

'It's the old Priory,' he muttered, his eyes taking on a funny look. 'Back in the _____ _____ they had to hide, those priests, or they'd get themselves executed.'

'What's a Priory?' I asked, scratching my red hair, and hoping that he would come back to the real world pretty soon. At the moment, I could tell, he was off Somewhere in History.

'In the time of Henry the Eighth, all priests were in danger of having their heads _____ ____,' said Sol, blinking behind his circular _____ . 'So they built priest holes to hide in secret passages that only **they** knew about.'

I tried to imagine what that had to do with Roger and a flat bit of stone in a field. There certainly wasn't anything left to put a secret passage in.

'I bet your dog is still missing at tea-time,' said Sol, _____ ___ _____ and looking irritatingly wise.

All day, I couldn't get my mind off Roger, probably scrambling around in some invisible secret passage leading right down to the centre of the earth. Poor Roger! He's probably met some real giant rabbits down there. Or the Lost Valley of the _____ , or something.

Sue came up to me at break.

'I've heard you've discovered an adventure,' she said.

'Something about a lost dog, and a _____ _____.'
I was surprised. Sue had never spoken to me before.

_____ as I'd fallen over in the last Sports Day sack race, and tripped her up. It was the first time she'd come second in anything.

'Well, I'm not sure, really,' I stuttered. 'It's Sol who made all that up.'

'Ah, but he **knows**,' said Sue. 'He knows about everything. So, I'll join you two later. Okay?'

Fit the correct words and phrases into the gaps in the passage.

freeze, frisky, chopped off, disappeared, stroking his chin, dinosaurs, secret passage, old days, spectacles, adventurer, squeeze, autumn, chocolate, especially.

Exercise 2

Roger hadn't come back by tea-time.

'Strange,' said Mum. 'He's never done that before!'

She was also surprised by the couple of friends I'd brought back. In the first place, I wasn't _____ with friends. The World's Worst Bungler, who could make blots with a biro, wasn't exactly the _____ _____ _____ around.

'This is Sue, and that's Solomon,' I'd said, and she'd looked carefully at the tall girl dressed in jeans and tartan shirt, and the small, _____ boy who followed me home.

'Solomon,' she'd said, nodding. 'Unusual name.'

She gave them some biscuits and a drink of Cola, then we went looking for Roger.

'Interesting,' said Sol, yet again, standing on the same patch and stroking his chin in that thoughtful way. 'Now, clearly, the passage can't run _____ because there is very little left of the building. Also, there is no clear opening that shows a vertical shaft, going down.'

I was just about to ask what on earth all that meant, when Sue _____ ____ _____.

'He's meaning,' she said, 'that the secret passage doesn't go along, and it doesn't go straight down.' She indicated with her hands.

'It's oblique,' said Sol. 'It goes down at an angle. It creates an illusion.'

Now, I've never been that good with words, so this _____ _____ was getting to me.

'Everything looks solid,' continued Sol, 'but the secret passage is there somewhere.'

'I suppose...,' said Sue, walking around and testing the ground.

I walked across the stone square. I was going to look for a rabbit hole. Those were much more real than stupid secret passages.

Then, I put my big, bungling feet into an _____ _____ and fell in.

Suddenly, it was like being on a long, long _____ at the fair. Except that I was sliding down in the dark.

'To the Centre of the Earth,' I heard myself saying. 'To the Land of Dinosaurs.'

Half way down to the Centre of the Earth, I hit something solid. Very solid. And it's very painful hitting something solid when you're a bag of bones like me.

'Bag of bones,' I said. I felt a cold nose _____ up to my cheek, and a long wet tongue licking my nose.

'Roger!' I muttered, ___ _____ . Down there, deep in the earth, it wasn't dark any more. There was a light coming from somewhere.

'There's a light, Roger,' I said, and he whined in my ear. 'Let's go and see where the light is coming from.'

We were in a narrow passage. At the end of it, daylight was _____ _____ , and that's what I wanted most of all now.

I could feel myself turning blue from fear already. Being locked in, _____ ___ _____ , as well as all those other things.

At the end of the passage I found a small room. High above, a narrow shaft of light lit up the whole place. It was a _____ room, full of old furniture.

'It smells of ghosts,' I said out loud.

'It does, doesn't it?' said a voice behind me.

Fit the correct words and phrases into the gaps in the passage.

filtering through, snuffling, scared to death, horizontally, angle business, helter-skelter, Einstein faced, overflowing, most popular person, interrupted my thoughts, open space, in relief, gloomy.

Exercise 3

There was a tapping from somewhere. __ ____ _____
about a sandy beach and the 'tap, tap' was _____
_____ _____ from it.

I woke up in the _____ of the bedroom, and sat
up. I could hear my heart _____ in the silence.

'Who's there?' I _____ , thinking that the noise was
coming from my bedroom door.

I heard the sound again. It was coming from the window.

Slowly, holding tight to the necklace in my left hand, I
climbed out of bed and stumbled across to the window, and
peered into the gloom outside.

There was a mist outside, a swirling fog lighted by the
moon. From out of the mist floated a figure in white, her eyes
sad, pleading, her skin bloodless. It was Rebecca. She tapped
on the window.

'Let me in,' she pleaded.

I hesitated for a second, but just for a second. I didn't
even ask myself what Rebecca was doing, floating outside my
window – fifteen feet ____ _____ _____ .

I opened the window, and the mist _____ in. With the
mist came a strange light. Rebecca floated in with it.

'Hello Blue,' she said. She smiled as she floated down to
stand before me.

'How did you do that, Rebecca?' I asked. It was a
_____ question. I knew that something was wrong.

'You know I'm not Rebecca, don't you?' said the white-
faced figure. The voice was changing.

'Who are you?' I asked.

Fear came rushing through my body. Her eyes, slowly changing colour from blue to green, were _____ me. She was growing taller, too, by the second, and those curly blonde locks were changing to black.

'Who are you?' I said again. I knew already who it was, but no different words came to mind.

She was tall now, like the first time I saw her.

'Come, now,' she said, reaching out a long bony hand. 'Give me the necklace, and I will leave you alone.' Her words hissed and _____ around in my head, as if both of us were standing in a deep cave.

'Go away,' I said to the Witch. 'Go away. You can't touch me.'

The face of the woman in front of me changed again. There was rage and cruelty in it now.

'I am Meliphanes, the Great Witch,' she hissed. 'Give it to me, you little _____.'

Her green eyes were furious _____ in her skull.

'No! No! No!' I screamed, clenching my fists and closing my eyes tight. 'Go away!'

There was a screaming roar, that _____ itself from in front of me and rocketed away through the open window. The window crashed shut, and left me once again in silence.

When I opened my eyes, all was black again. I groped my way back to the bed, climbed under the bedclothes, and fell into an _____ sleep.

Fit the correct words and phrases into the gaps in the passage.

pinpoints, echoed, worm, hypnotising, swirled, foolish, off the ground, pitch-black, I was dreaming, pounding, dragging me away, launched, exhausted, croaked.

Exercise 4

The following is a passage in the book about a 'Tell'. The three children are discussing how to escape from the Great Witch, who can read Blue's mind.

She turned and began to walk towards the door of the church. Then, she stopped and turned back to us.

'Just a minute,' she said, 'we're at ___ _____here. The Witch is _____ _____ _____ , Blue. She knows exactly our _____ _____ _____ . Every word we speak is _____ to her through your thoughts.'

I hung my head.

'I'm sorry,' I said.

'Don't worry,' said Sue. 'Have you heard of a 'tell?' Sol and I looked at each other.

'What's that?' asked Sol.

'It's something that gives away what you are really thinking,' said Sue. 'For example, you say something, and I try to decide whether what you are saying is the truth or a lie.'

'How can you do that?' I asked.

'You look for _____ signs,' said Sue. 'When people lie, they often don't look straight at the person they're lying to, or they scratch their nose – something like that.'

'I see,' said Sol, 'but what has this got to do with the Witch?'

'This.' said Sue. 'We make two plans – Plan A and Plan B. One is a _____ , the other is the one we do.'

'Tell us the plans,' I said, knowing that the Witch would be listening.

'Plan A,' said Sue, 'is to separate as soon as we leave the church. We each go down the paths that separate at the front door, for the road, the river and the graveyard.'

'And Plan B?' asked Sol.

'Plan B is to stay together and battle our way to the roadway. Okay?'

Sol and I nodded, and Sue led the way to the main door. Outside, we both looked at her.

'Which Plan?' I said.

'Neither,' said Sue, pointing to the river path. 'Just run!' We _____ like mad towards the river until, directly ahead of us, two gigantic figures lumbered into our path.

'Now,' shouted Sue, 'together – "Depart to the risen dead!"' She raised her Alpha Weapon, and we followed suit.

'Fire!' yelled Sue. The _____ was marvellous to behold. First one Being, and then the next, was blasted into eternity once more by Alpha Power.

We moved on, down to the river bank and along the _____ back to our own estate.

'What about all that stuff about Plan A and Plan B?' I

asked. 'We did something completely different.'

'It's called Double Bluff,' said Sue. 'We had to separate the Witch's forces. She knows that I had already told you to stick together. So, Plan A is the most likely, but she has to cover for Plan B, and sends a small force to each of the pathways. When we all went down one, our Power _____ what she had in store for us.'

'Brilliant!' said Sol.

'My Mum calls it _____ _____ ,' said Sue.

'We simply used the Witch's greatest strength to our advantage. She seems to have the advantage when she can read Blue's thoughts. Now that will work to our advantage. In the future she will never know if we are bluffing or not.'

Fit the correct words and phrases into the gaps in the passage.

common sense, destruction, a disadvantage, reading your mind, relayed, strengths and weaknesses, bluff, tell-tale, bridleway, scampered, outnumbered.

8 Word Searches and More Reading Passages

Advanced readers at the upper age range (10–11 years) whom this book is concerned with, need reading passages to stretch their abilities. These sometimes extend into the realms of 'boring' (according to some), but the ability to easily consume such areas of reading will enable them to read and understand longer and more meaningful novels, some from the past using quite difficult text.

Word searches help word recognition to a certain extent, and are much liked by most age groups. They may also encourage a love of words, and such motivation should not be lightly dismissed.

WORD SEARCHES

Word search 1

Find these words:

ancient	surprise	conversation
disease	miserable	council
lightning	stationary	stationery
principle	principal	

```
C  O  N  V  E  R  S  T  A  T  I  O
C  S  T  A  T  I  O  N  A  R  Y  P
O  N  L  I  G  H  T  N  I  N  G  R
N  S  T  A  T  G  H  I  T  I  O  I
V  L  I  G  A  N  C  I  E  N  T  N
E  Y  P  R  I  N  C  A  N  C  I  E
R  R  L  P  R  I  N  C  I  P  L  E
S  E  I  G  D  I  S  E  A  S  M  C
A  N  D  I  S  E  A  S  E  T  I  O
T  O  H  T  P  R  I  N  C  A  S  U
I  I  M  I  S  E  R  A  B  L  E  N
O  T  I  O  S  U  R  P  R  A  B  C
N  A  S  U  R  P  R  I  S  E  N  I
S  T  C  O  N  V  E  R  S  N  I  L
T  S  C  P  R  I  N  C  I  P  A  L
```

Word search 2 – Scientific words

Find these words:

laboratory	chemical	beaker
spatula	potassium	hydrogen
zinc	balance	carbonate
oxygen	stomach	kidney

```
B  A  L  P  O  T  A  H  Y  D
B  I  N  C  S  T  O  M  A  N
A  O  S  B  A  L  A  N  C  E
L  X  T  C  H  K  P  C  A  G
A  Y  O  L  Y  I  O  N  T  O
N  G  M  A  D  D  T  I  E  R
S  P  A  T  U  L  A  Z  C  D
S  P  C  C  A  E  S  O  B  Y
A  N  H  R  B  Y  S  N  E  H
B  A  C  H  E  M  I  C  A  L
A  O  X  Y  G  Z  U  I  K  N
B  E  A  K  K  I  M  C  E  C
L  A  B  O  R  A  T  O  R  Y
O  X  Y  G  E  N  C  N  I  Y
C  L  N  E  Y  D  I  K  E  Y
A  C  A  R  B  O  N  A  T  E
R  S  P  A  T  C  A  R  B  N
B  B  Y  E  N  D  I  K  K  D
```

Word search 3 – Countries, festivals and times of the year

Find these words:

Luxembourg	Pakistan	England
Singapore	France	Christmas
Easter	Eid	Diwali
Germany	Australia	Summer
Autumn	Peru	Uruguay
Chad		

```
F  R  A  N  C  E  L  G  A  N
F  F  R  A  H  F  U  S  I  N
R  I  C  H  R  E  T  S  A  E
S  L  E  D  I  A  Y  A  S  A
P  A  K  I  S  T  A  N  U  E
E  W  I  E  T  S  U  A  M  R
I  I  D  I  M  T  G  U  M  O
N  D  C  H  A  D  U  S  E  P
U  P  E  R  S  U  R  A  R  A
C  H  R  I  S  R  U  I  D  G
Y  N  A  M  R  E  G  L  I  N
M  A  N  G  I  P  L  A  W  I
D  N  A  L  G  N  E  R  A  S
E  A  C  H  R  I  S  T  M  A
S  G  V  R  U  A  K  S  C  H
L  U  X  E  M  B  O  U  R  G
T  E  N  M  U  T  U  A  H  C
D  L  A  G  N  E  P  U  E  R
```

Word search 4 – Animals

Find these words:

armadillo	buffalo	giraffe
budgerigar	albatross	hippopotamus
leopard	llama	chaffinch
kingfisher	pheasant	pigeon
dachshund	mackerel	eel
elk	yak	wren owl

```
A R M A P B V F Y G I E T
B L A A H G I R A F F E R
U L L B E L K T K R O L O
D A R M A D I L L O C A S
G M P A S P N L A W H L S
E A I C A O G L M L S B A
S D G K N P F P A D O A H
U A E E T P I O R N K T C
M C E R Y I S E D U L R N
A H E E K H H L C H L O I
T S K L A P E N H S N S F
O P H E A I R I A H E S F
P S A N D G W L F C R S A
O B U D G E R I G A R L H
P P H L E O P A R D L L C
P E W R E N C H E P C H K
I B U F F A L O O W E W Y
H W R N E Y K A N E S W A
A C H K E L E R P H T R C
```

HARDER READING PASSAGES AND QUESTIONS
Test 1
Read the passage and answer the questions

It was difficult to get helpers for the afternoon shift, so Miss Smith took it on every day. She said that it was a small way of repaying all the kindness she had received in her beloved adopted Country... She never wanted to go anywhere else or do anything else and she had no friends. She kept the Vicarage in perfect order and cooked succulent meals out of nothing at all. Mrs Monks called her a 'treasure' and left it at that. It wasn't until Mrs Mason came to the village that the limelight began to fall upon Miss Smith.

Mrs Mason's journalistic genius had so far functioned chiefly in the atmosphere of Bloomsbury, but removal to the country seemed to have given it fresh impetus, and after a week or two, having exhausted every other topic connected with the village, she fell upon Miss Smith, the Grateful Refugee. Mrs Mason pursued her indefatigably, interviewing her on her suffering in her native land and on those feelings of gratitude to her adopted country that found such constant outlet in sea boot stockings and the local canteen. And then – when one would have thought that she had said all that could possibly be said on the subject – she discovered Miss Smith's soldier. Miss Smith's soldier was a tall stooping military-looking man, with a white moustache and limp, who had moved from London at the beginning of the war and lived in rooms in Hadley. He took a 'constitutional' into the country every afternoon, walking slowly and leaning heavily on his stick, and, passing the canteen, would often go in for a rest before continuing his walk. And Miss Smith adopted him. He became her soldier. He was a silent, reserved man, but questioning would draw from him an account of how he had been gassed and shot through the spine in the last war... and to Miss Smith he typified all the other soldiers who had suffered these things for her freedom.

Moreover, he had been a prisoner of war in Germany and could speak a little German, which he practiced with shy pride upon Miss Smith. Miss Smith discovered that he had been born in Yorkshire and that one of his happiest memories was the Yorkshire tea-cakes that his mother used to make... He had never tasted anything to compare with them, he said, since he came... So, in order to give him a pleasant surprise, Miss Smith set to work to make a Yorkshire tea-cake. She hunted through recipe books; she experimented on the Vicarage gas cooker... until she had at last made a Yorkshire tea-cake that she considered fit to be offered to him. And he pronounced it good – as good, in fact, as the tea-cakes his mother used to make. Miss Smith's gratitude was unbounded, and thereafter, whenever the soldier stopped at the canteen, Miss Smith would have a tea-cake ready for him to take home with him.

Mrs Mason seized the story with zest and wrote an article – Fraulein Schmitt, the Soldier and the Tea-cakes – which appeared in one of the monthly reviews. After that, having exhausted every other subject, she took refuge in those happy hunting grounds of the journalist – War-time Cookery and The Mistakes Our Generals Have Made in Every Theatre of the War – and Miss Smith relapsed into oblivion.

Not entirely into oblivion, however, for the story of the tea-cake had somehow struck the popular imagination. Even Mrs Brown, harassed as she was by points and coupons, by the curious appearance of war-time sausages and the still more curious disappearance of war-time eggs, found time to turn up an old cookery book and make a Yorkshire tea-cake.

(*William at War*, Richmal Crompton)

Questions

1 How many different people are mentioned in the text?
2 What is Mrs Mason's job?
3 What is Miss Smith's job?
4 Where was Miss Smith's soldier from, and where does he live now? Where was he born?
5 What did Miss Smith do for the soldier? What was his response?
6 What was the result of the article that Mrs Mason wrote?

What do these words mean in the passage:

limelight   atmosphere   impetus

indefatigably   constitutional   gratification

oblivion

Test 2

Read the passage and answer the questions

Rebecca reached the school gate and stopped, feeling a little bewildered. The heavy, iron gates of the school were closed, though not locked. She looked around her, missing the warmth of congenial company, hoping for the sight of a familiar face. It was not Saturday or Sunday, she was sure of that, yet the school grounds were completely empty, the borders overgrown, paths left unswept, the stonework and paint of the buildings faded.

She pushed at the heavy, iron gates, surprised at the effort needed to open them, and bewildered by the flaking paint and ingrained rust on the metalwork. Yesterday, surely, these gates had been as clean as a whistle, newly painted green, a shocking colour but, with the neatly trimmed borders and newly mown lawns, giving the school an air of spruceness and elegance.

Wearily, Rebecca picked her way along the litter-strewn path to the school's main door. Tentatively she pushed it open and revealed the long, familiar corridor, now carpetless and dusty. She stepped inside and stood for a moment, listening to the hollow silence, and then moved on towards the Great Hall. Where, where was everybody? Where were the furnishings of yesterday?

(*Time Lapse*, Ken Adams)

Questions
1 Why was Rebecca so bewildered?
2 Write down the words and phrases that describe the state of the place on this day.
3 What was inside the school, and why was that so surprising?

Find the meanings of these words in the passage:
bewildered   congenial   ingrained   spruceness
elegance   tentatively   hollow

Test 3

Read the passage and answer the questions

At half past nine that night Tom and Sid were sent to bed as usual. They said their prayers, and Sid was soon asleep. Tom lay awake and waited in restless impatience. When it seemed to him that it must be nearly daylight, he heard the clock strike ten! This was despair. He would have tossed and fidgeted, as his nerves demanded, but he was afraid he might wake Sid. So he lay still and stared up into the dark. Everything was dismally still. By-and-by, out of the stillness, little scarcely perceptible noises began to emphasize themselves. The ticking of the clock began to bring itself to notice. Old beams began to crack mysteriously. The stairs creaked faintly. Evidently spirits were abroad. A measured, muffled snore issued from Aunt Polly's chamber.

And now the tiresome chirping of a cricket that no human ingenuity could locate began. Next the ghastly ticking of a death-watch in the wall at the bed's head made Tom shudder – it meant that somebody's days were numbered. Then the howl of a far-off dog rose on the night air and was answered by a fainter howl from a remoter distance. Tom was in an agony. At last he was satisfied that time had ceased and eternity begun; he began to doze in spite of himself; the clock chimed eleven, but he did not hear it.

(The Adventures of Tom Sawyer, Mark Twain)

Questions

1 What noises were there in the night as Tom lay awake?

2 What did the sound of the death-watch beetle mean?

3 Why was Tom 'in an agony'?

4 What happened to stop Tom hear the clock chime eleven?

Find the meanings of these words in the passage:

despair	fidgeted	scarcely
perceptible	emphasize	tiresome
chirping	ingenuity	muffled
measured	eternity	doze